POEMS: BY ROBERT HUGH BENSON

Robert Hugh Benson.

❧ POEMS ❧

BY ROBERT HUGH BENSON

LONDON
BURNS AND OATES
28 ORCHARD STREET
W

P
B

First Impression, December 1914
Second Impression, January 1915 .
Third Impression, February 1915

A NOTE OF INTRODUCTION BY WILFRID MEYNELL

❧ CONTENTS

ROBERT HUGH BENSON

THE death of Robert Hugh Benson in the October of 1914 came as a grief and a loss which even war-time and the long roll of heroic dead could not diminish or obscure. Yet those who were bound to him by ties of spiritual as well as personal affection had at least this consolation, that such ties are of all the most enduring; and that he who had brought them on earth very near to Heaven would in Heaven be very near to them on earth. And to that intimate company were joined a multitude who knew him only by what he had publicly done and written and spoken, and whose feeling was fitly represented by a girl who, hearing he had gone, was silent and then said, "One feels as if one had lost a near relation"—something closer than a friend. Even so there was this reprieve —he was a relative who had left to all of us a legacy, an example for an inheritance.

For, if it seems that the loss of the active man of fine talents is the irreparable one, let this at least be our comfort that his activities go on to a continual harvesting. Robert Hugh Benson, dying at the age of forty-three, achieved more in that short span than it is commonly given to the longest career to put to its account. The eleven years of his Catholic life, judged by its labours, might be called, in the poet's phrase, eleven years of years. A complete subjugation of the will was his note ; and one of its evidences was the unflagging labour of his pen, which he was therefore able to pledge to half-incredulous publishers in advance, with a certainty of performance. What that exacted drudgery cost a man whose business was in some sort his sensitiveness of apprehension, and who had, as it were, to yield to his moods in order to make his "copy," perhaps only writers of his own standing can appreciate. Certain it is that no such strain can be made without imminent danger of a snapping. A kite may flap idly in the air with a long bedraggled life that achieves nothing. But an air-machine, such as those with which the author of the "Lord of the World" filled our atmosphere, has, with a higher and purposeful flight, a more disastrous downfall. The small hitch deals out death and destruc-

14

tion. Mgr. Benson knew that the high flight meant the annihilating fall, and, looking into " the bright face of danger," he did not shrink from the track his sense of duty and service marked out for him. Why should he have shrunk, believing what he believed, and being, besides, logical? It was characteristic of him, as a man who was at once all things to all men, and nothing to any man, that, only a few months before the end, when a lady asked to read his hand, he gave it to her; and, on being told that he would die before he was fifty, exclaimed, " What good news ! "

When Robert Hugh Benson, after days at Eton and Cambridge, after ordination, parish experience and an attempt at Community life as an Anglican, entered the Catholic Church, he was only thirty-two, and had given little or no public sign of the mental and spiritual development possible to him. It might have been not unreasonably supposed that he would depend for his importance on the paradox of his position—that of the first son of an English Primate, barring only Toby Matthew, to become a Catholic. He might count upon a success of curiosity; his lot that of a handy substitute to open

15

a bazaar the day her ladyship was so provokingly lacking. The boyish manner of the young blue-eyed, blond-haired neophyte perhaps favoured the notion of his abandonment to such a fate. And it is the test and triumph of Mgr. Benson's achievements that his origin was swiftly forgotten in his own originality, and that he became far too eminent in himself to be thought or spoken of any more as his eminent father's son.

These activities, that did not rely on mere impulse, and that, therefore, cost him dearly, were all-embracing, public and private, undertaken always with one purpose—helpfulness to others. To this end, difficulties existed only to be overcome. One of his brothers tells of Robert Hugh that, in childhood, he was afraid to enter a dark room, and, on being asked why, said, "I see b—b—blood." That shrinking from the unknown, translated in after-life into a thousand and one reluctances to confront strange things, strange places, strange faces, he utterly extinguished in himself, just as he fought down hesitations of manner, and never allowed defects of delivery to lessen by one his appearances in the pulpit or on

the platform. Conferences could never be dead
things when he was there to give them life—to
give them literally, as we now reckon, his own life.
The absence in him of all desire to shine, of all the
vanity which severe moralists like Manning sensi-
tively suspect in the popular preacher, allowed him,
nevertheless, on any serviceable private occasion, to
talk about the last thing he wanted to think about,
himself. The multitude of people he instructed
into the Church—men of the world, noble-hearted
women not a few, undergraduates whom they
called "Bensonians" at Cambridge—heard from
him about his own ways and byways into the
Heavenly Jerusalem. They knew that as an
Anglican clergyman he had heard confessions
constantly, and had regarded the confessional then
with exactly the same reverence and sanctity that
a Catholic brought to it; and that he had told his
rosary like any nun. They knew that he had already
turned aside from the Higher Critics to the man in
the street, for whom "The Religion of the Plain
Man" was afterwards indited; and, in this relation,
it is worth noting that he just lived long enough to
see Professor von Harnack, confident interpreter of

B

ancient documents, giving a grotesque travesty of current ones which the said Plain Man who runs may read. Nor did Mgr. Benson refrain from acknowledging, even to those who classed it with Wardour Street literature, that " John Inglesant " obtained a powerful hold on his young imagination, and ranked among the commanding influences that brought him into the Church. His matured taste turned otherwhere perhaps ; for he came to the opinion that Francis Thompson's " Hound of Heaven " was the most valuable auxiliary of the missionary priest in his work for the conversion of England.

And always at the end of all recountings came the profession :—" Every single day of my life I thank God more and more that I am a Catholic." Every single day, too, that thankfulness was made manifest in more than speech. His labours, easily within the recollection of all who read, need here no enumeration. If he was not composing a novel with a purpose, he was compiling a prayer-book or writing a mystery-play, or a comedy for the professional stage, which ecclesiastic rule would not permit him to see performed ; or he was talking at street corners—the vanguard indeed ; or he was preaching a course of sermons in Rome or London, or, as at the last hour, in Salford ; or he was instructing and receiving converts, or going far afield to baptize somebody's baby to please a young mother, or conferring with an aged invalid to please a daughter ; or lecturing, or writing verses, which are in themselves a revelation of his character, a revelation which in this volume is now publicly made ; or he was eagerly investigating psychic phenomena ; or, in what to him were hours of idleness, devising a scheme for a Catholic colony, or carving, or decorating with his own hand his interesting Hare Street House at Buntingford. There he learned tapestry weaving; and to complete the panels that record *The Dance of Death*, he designed yet one more in which Death meets Robert Hugh Benson.

Of his services to charitable institutions we need make no record except this—that he had an impersonal partiality for—all of them. Yet one may be named apart, the Homes of Mr. Norman Potter, since it was for their benefit that he put into the market the autobiographical and heart-searching poems here printed. They are very intimate ; and as such are proper to poetry even in the case of a writer who had not specially studied the mechanism of poetry as his medium. Under cover of poetical convention, he is able to bare himself, equally in the lines written before he became a Catholic in 1903, and in "The Priest's Lament" of a later date. In "Christian Evidences" he gets back to his intuitions; to that which made him, ardent investigator though he was, ever in closer touch with the simple than with the scientific—back to that *witness within himself* which Christ promises and gives to all His own; while in "Visions of the Night" we are at close quarters with that apprehensiveness which, while it imposed suffering, also conferred insight— the insight by which others learned to see. One passage in "Savonarola Moriturus" is especially self-revealing, and that for a reason it is now no breach of decorum to set forth. A year or two before his death he talked with a neophyte on the sacrifices one might have to make for the Faith. "And are you sure you would make them all?" he was asked. His reply was that he would like to say "Yes," but that he dare not answer for what he might be made to yield under bodily torture. The first four lines of the second stanza of the Savonarola poem are the more poignant for this modesty of the author's own estimate of his powers of endurance, powers which he thenceforth put to sharp apprenticeship and test, passing out, not vanquished, but victor.

Of his novels I do not here attempt an appreciation. As a ruthless writer, where ruthlessness comes into the scheme of a man's salvation, as it had been in that of his own, let him be ranked. In the spiritual warfare he gave no quarter. Whether he was cruel, besides, in the burning of *The Coward*, who makes indeed cowards of us all; whether he views woman as no more than an adjunct of man, an accident for the hindering or the helping of his salvation; whether Dorothy is properly killed so that Roger Mallock may prove his vocation; these, and many more, are the problems that palpitate in his pages, and that men and women, according to their varied experiences, will variously adjudge. Of his historical novels in general he was inclined to say very much what he said of "Come Rack, Come Rope": "I fear it is the kind of book which anyone acquainted with the history, manners, and customs of the Elizabethan age should find no difficulty in writing." If, in this class, the author proved conspicuously his industry and his facility—uncommon but not rare faculties —then in "Initiation" and other studies of current life he was nothing if not individual. In these he was of his age and no other; he was himself and no other. Nor were the sensitivenesses of these books without their effect on the whole of his productions. When in historical romance he described a martyrdom, we have also his own comment on it: "It seems to me, who have never been on the rack, that I have succeeded pretty well in writing down what the rack must have felt like, and the mental states it must have induced. When I had finished writing that scene, I was conscious of very distinct, even slightly painful, sensations in my own wrists and ankles." Obviously there was an apprehension, necessary for one class of book, which greatly benefited the other; and the experience of the hero in "Initiation" could not have been conveyed, had not the author himself gone under an anæsthetic in a nursing home; and again endured another ordeal without an opiate, "to learn what pain really was"—a sharp lesson of

sixty hours. Similarly the description of the head-
aches of the hero (how real a hero !) in "Initiation," the most vivid description of its class
in all English literature, could only have been
written by one who had himself suffered them,
and suffered them with a sensibility that is fortu-
nately the iron crown conferred upon only the very
elect.

To be so capable of suffering and yet to face
it, and, as we might say in the instance just
given, to waylay it and embrace it—that is one
of the many marvels of Mgr. Benson's quickly-
ended—or never to be ended—career. Fit with
his perpetual sense of detachment was his death
far from his home. Failure of the heart was the
final paradox in the history of a man whose
heart had never failed him before, were a hurt
soul to be healed, or an uncovenanted kindness
to be done.

"He maketh His ministers a flame of fire."
Knowing the minister, we infer the flame. But
with many—and notably with Robert Hugh Benson
—there is the double and responsive signal—the
flame proclaims the minister. And because he

23

sought every breeze that fanned that fire, and because he made haste to diffuse the light and the warmth till he burnt himself out, his very ashes shall be held as a sacred trust.

W. M.

POEMS

LINES

I CANNOT soar and sing my Lord and love;
    No eagle's wings have I,
No power to rise and greet my King above,
    No heart to fly.
Creative Lord Incarnate, let me lean
    My heavy self on Thee;
Nor let my utter weakness come between
    Thy strength and me.

I cannot trace Thy Providence and plan,
    Nor dimly comprehend
What in Thyself Thou art, and what is man,
    And what the end.
Here in this wilderness I cannot find
    The path the Wise Men trod;
Grant me to rest on Thee, Incarnate Mind
    And Word of God.

I cannot love, my heart is turned within
    And locked within; (Ah me!
How shivering in self-love I sit) for sin
    Has lost the key.

Ah ! Sacred Heart of Jesus, Flame divine,
 Ardent with great desire,
My hope is set upon that love of Thine,
 Deep Well of Fire.

I cannot live alone another hour ;
 Jesu, be Thou my Life !
I have not power to strive ; be Thou my Power
 In every strife !
I can do nothing—hope, nor love, nor fear,
 But only fail and fall.
Be Thou my soul and self, O Jesu dear,
 My God and all !

A HALT

LIE still, my soul, the Sun of Grace
    Is warm within this garden space
        Beneath tall kindly trees.
The quiet light is green and fair ;
A fragrance fills the swooning air ;
        Lie still, and take thine ease.

This silent noon of Jesu's love
Is warm about thee and above—
        A tender Lord is He.
Lie still an hour—this place is His.
He has a thousand pleasaunces,
And each all fair and fragrant is,
        And each is all for thee.

Then, Jesu, for a little space
I rest me in this garden place,
        All sweet to scent and sight.
Here, from this high-road scarce withdrawn,
I thrust my hot hands in the lawn
Cool yet with dew of far-off dawn
        And saturate with light.

But ah, dear Saviour, human-wise,
I yearn to pierce all mysteries,
To catch Thine Hands, and see Thine Eyes
    When evening sounds begin.
There, in Thy white Robe, Thou wilt wait
At dusk beside some orchard gate,
And smile to see me come so late,
    And, smiling, call me in.

PATIENCE

I

I WAITED for the Lord a little space.
  So little ! in whose sight as yesterday
Passes a thousand years :—I cried for grace,
    Impatient of delay.

II

He waited for me—ah so long ! For He
  Sees in one single day a loss or gain
That bears a fruit through all eternity :—
    My soul, did He complain ?

I

AT PRAYER MEETING

THOU who hast made these hearts to
    answer Thine,—
      Infused Thy virtues, faith, hope,
    charity,
Mirror'd Thine image here that all may see,
If such be earthly, what must be divine ;
Thou who hast taught by riddle, type, and sign,
    The weakness of our immaturity
    The measure of Thy strength one day to be,
By precept upon precept, line on line ;—

Lord, take these sighs and longings, hopes and
    fears,
    The throb of love, the pulse of penitence,
    The praise of all Thy love has done—shall do—
And teach us,—as Thy fuller light appears
    And brightens at the gates of earthly sense,—
Who love Thy grace, to love Thy glory too.

II
AT HIGH MASS

THOU Who hast made this world so won-
    drous fair ;—
      The pomp of clouds ; the glory of the
    sea ;
  Music of water ; song-birds' melody ;
The organ of Thy thunder in the air ;
Breath of the rose ; and beauty everywhere—
  Lord, take this stately service done to Thee,
  The grave enactment of Thy Calvary
In jewelled pomp and splendour pictured there !

Lord, take the sounds and sights ; the silk and gold;
  The white and scarlet ; take the reverent grace
  Of ordered step ; window and glowing wall—
Prophet and Prelate, holy men of old ;
  And teach us children of the Holy Place
Who love Thy Courts, to love Thee best of all.

VISIONS OF THE NIGHT

LIBERA ME A TERRORE NOCTURNO A NEGOTIO
PERAMBULANTE IN TENEBRIS . . . CUSTODI
ANIMAM MEAM O DOMINE VISITANS ME VISI-
TATIONE SANCTORUM REVELA MIHI ANIMUM
IN VISIONIBUS NOCTIS

ERE yet I slept, the summer night
    Lay vague and mellow in the gloom
    Beyond the steady candlelight.
The moth came tapping on the pane,
    Intent on doom.
Then sank into the night again.

Then, as I lie, the darkened walls
   Grow dim ; the sheets are turned to air,
As fold on fold the slumber falls.
    The ticking clock grows dumb with sleep ;
      And everywhere
About the soul slow pauses creep.

The sense contracts from form and space—
   Shrinks to a speck within the brain—
Then opens on a wider place
   That knows no law, no harmony ;
     Till once again
A newer world is born for me.

34

My spirit moves in dark dismay
   About a house of misty halls :
I hear the shuddering branches sway
   At gable-corners ; on the floor
      And on the walls
The firelight glimmers through the door.

I sit and talk beside the bed,
   Grasp hands, and meet the living eyes,
Of one whom I had fancied dead
   Some ten years back : " How strange," I say
      In glad surprise,
" That we should meet again to-day ! "

He smiles for answer : sudden then
   I understand the mystery
Of dying, for the sons of men ;
   And wonder where the sadness lay
      To see him die
Last year—or was it yesterday ?

All passes ;—down long corridors,
   That lead about this wilderness,
Fall footsteps tramping on the floors,
   That come from nowhere and are gone ;
      Yet none the less
I run in panting terror on.

Here is a lawn with beds and grass ;
   The birds sing shrilly in the air,
While multitudes pass and re-pass,
    Who fill me with unknown distress,
       That holds me there
To mark their swift unweariedness.

And so with eyes that ache to close,
   And feet that fly and flag in turn,
About, about, my spirit goes.
    In wondrous wise from deep to deep,
       Before me burn
The crumbling pageantries of sleep.

O Lord of Light, who gav'st me breath,
   And set'st my spirit ill at ease
Within the body of this death,
    What means this dreaming rush and rout—
       These phantasies
Born from within and seen without ?

Since ghost and devil, foe and friend
   Throng—shadows on this shadow-stage—
Move from no source and seek no end—
    Since all the passions born of fear
       Terror and rage,
As in a looking-glass appear ;

Why com'st Thou not Thyself, O Lord,
  To still the tossing of the brain,
And calm with one imperious word
   This storm of fancy under Thee,
      And yet again
Bid peace, as once in Galilee ?

Come, Lord ; and if through toilsome days
  I pray in dumb perplexity,
And strive to lift my wearied praise,—
   Yet let me rest when night is deep,
      And look on Thee
The Lord of waking and of sleep.

PLEAD THOU MY CAUSE !

I

ATTRITION

PLEAD Thou my cause, else who will plead
    for me,
    My Kingly Advocate before the Throne ?
Trembling I stand ; guilty, ashamed, alone,
Girt only by my own iniquity,
Cried down by sins that fain would silence Thee,
    Some coming after, some to judgment gone.
    What I have done, what I have left undone,
Beckon me out to deathless misery.

    The Court is set, and will not let me go ;
        The heavy books are black with blotted shame.
        I cannot answer ; none can plead but Thou.
I knew not what I did in sinning so ;
        Hell hungers for me ; see, the worm, the flame !
        Nought but Love's eloquence can save me
        now.

II

CONTRITION

PLEAD Thou my cause ; yet let me bear the
        pain,
    Lord, Who hast done so much to ransom me,
Now that I know how I have wounded Thee,
And crucified Thee, Prince of Life, again.
Yea, let me suffer ; Thou wilt not disdain
    To let me hang beside Thee on the Tree
    And taste Thy bitter Cup of agony.
Let it not be that Thou hast died in vain.

Ah, awful Face of Love, bruised by my hand,
    Turn to me, pierce me with Thine eyes of
        flame,
        And give me deeper knowledge of my sin.
    So let me grieve ; and, when I understand
        How great my guilt, my ruin, and my shame,
        Open Thy Sacred Heart and let me in !

THE INVITATION

LORD take Thine ease within my heart,
    Rest here and count Thyself at home ;
    Do as Thou wilt ; rise, set, depart ;
My Master, not my guest, Thou art ;
  Come as Thou wilt, but come, Lord, come.

Do Thine own pleasure. Surely, Lord,
  Thou art full free to come and go,
To lift my sorrow by a word,
Or pierce me with a sudden sword,
  And leave me sobbing in my woe.

Come in broad day, for good or ill,
  In time of business or of prayer ;
Come in disguise, if so Thy Will
Be better served, that I may still
  Wait on my Lord, though unaware.

Come with the dawn, shine in on me
  And wake my soul with welcome light ;
Or let the twilight herald Thee,
And falling dusk Thy shelter be
  To shroud Thy coming from my sight.

Come by the way beneath the trees
　　Where whispering heath and bracken stir ;
There, where my spirit takes her ease,
Let that pure scented evening breeze
　　Waft me the aloes and the myrrh.

Come, tender Lover, still and bright,
　　Rose crowned and framed in gracious form ;
Or come with terror, and by night,
Thundrous and girt with vivid light,
　　A giant striding with the storm.

Come through the Cloister, past the lawn
　　And laurels where the thin jet plays ;
Where, from the wrangling world withdrawn,
Waking to silence dawn by dawn,
　　My soul comes forth to studious days.

Come through the carven door, and bring
　　A burst of Music through to me ;
One chord of organ-thundering
And measured song of those that sing,
　　Dear Saviour, to the praise of Thee.

Or come by some forgotten way
　　Untrodden long and overgrown ;
And on a sudden on a day
Burst in ; snap web and ivy spray
　　That claim the entrance for their own.

So many doors, and all divine,
    And every latch is loose to Thee ;
So many paths, and all are Thine
That bring Thee to this heart of mine,
    And all are therefore dear to me !

THE TERESIAN CONTEMPLATIVE

SHE moves in tumult ; round her lies
 The silence of the world of grace ;
 The twilight of our mysteries
Shines like high noonday on her face ;
Our piteous guesses, dim with fears,
She touches, handles, sees, and hears.

In her all longings mix and meet ;
 Dumb souls through her are eloquent ;
She feels the world beneath her feet
 Thrill in a passionate intent ;
Through her our tides of feeling roll
And find their God within her soul.

Her faith the awful Face of God
 Brightens and blinds with utter light ;
Her footsteps fall where late He trod ;
 She sinks in roaring voids of night ;
Cries to her Lord in black despair,
And knows, yet knows not, He is there.

A willing sacrifice she takes
    The burden of our fall within ;
Holy she stands ; while on her breaks
    The lightning of the wrath of sin ;
She drinks her Saviour's cup of pain,
And, one with Jesus, thirsts again.

O DEUS EGO AMO TE

O GOD, I love Thee mightily,
      Not only for Thy saving me,
      Nor yet because who love not Thee
Must burn throughout eternity.
Thou, Thou, my Jesu, once didst me
Embrace upon the bitter Tree.
For me the nails, the soldier's spear,
With injury and insult, bear—
In pain all pain exceeding,
In sweating and in bleeding,
Yea, very death, and that for me
      A sinner all unheeding !
O Jesu, should I not love Thee
Who thus hast dealt so lovingly—
Not hoping some reward to see,
Nor lest I my damnation be ;
But, as Thyself hast lovèd me,
So love I now and always Thee,
Because my King alone Thou art,
Because, O God, mine own Thou art !

FULFILMENT

FECISTI NOS AD TE ET INQUIETUM EST COR
NOSTRUM DONEC REQUIESCAT IN TE

THE City wakes to fever once again,
    Breathes up her smoke, and restless lies
      below,
Thirsty for life and eager of her pain;
    See, as the sun goes down
    How all the slumbrous town
Tosses her craving fingers to and fro!

The sobbing child that breaks her heart at sin,
    The fool self-centred at his solemn play,
The saint that dies without, the knave within,
    Each adds a note, and dies;
    While all about them rise
The crashing discords of a world's dismay.

Come, lift thine eyes from out this dark unrest
    Beyond the bitter mist of tears and blood!
Above the vivid fury of the west,
    With radiance softly keen,
    Incredibly serene,
A star swims high above the phantom flood,

Till in an ordered glory, star by star,
   Leaps into life the wonder of the sky ;
And in dark vaults, immeasurably far,
       The splendour spreads and breaks,
       And all wide heaven awakes
And earth's disorders and her tumults die.

Come, lift thine eyes from that disordered heart—
   Pities and passions, half-born treacheries,
Follies and sudden prudence—come apart
       And watch the dark unfold
       Her myriad gates of gold
Till all thy wailing into wonder dies !

So to the soul that, weary of her pain,
   Looks for her Lord in uttermost despair,
He spreads a vision of Himself again ;—
       Kindles her ancient creed,
       Lightens the dark indeed,
And writes Himself in glory everywhere.

Here throbs a heart that only lives for love,
   For warmth and colour, passion and desire,
Cries out for these alone :—and, lo above,
       Opens a vision dim—
       Wide Arms that yearn for him,
Eyes full of longing and a Heart of fire.

Here dwells a subtle mind that seeks to trace
   In line on line a symmetry and plan,
To mark degrees of glory and of grace :—
      And, lo, all wisdom lies
      Within the tranquil Eyes
Of that Incarnate Word that dwelt with man.

Here lives a soul that kindles at a tale
   Of noble deeds and daring, fair to see,
For very love of fighting glad to fail ;—
      And, lo, the hard-won throne
      Of Him that went alone
To win it, and a crown, on Calvary.

Lo, to the soul that looked for peace on earth,
   And lost her yearning with the barren years,
There dawns the Star that lit the Saviour's Birth—
      Broadens, until four-square,
      Gem-built and jewelled fair,
As once to John, the Peace of God appears.

Nay, but the veriest sinner in his sin
   Seeks but to clasp the life he knows is there,
Driv'n reckless by the power of God within :—
      Yet he may rise and gain
      Some harvest of his pain,
As Peter rose to pardon through despair.

FULFILMENT

Ah, God is good, Who writes His glory plain
   Above thee, and about thee at thy side,—
Bids thee look upward from that blinding pain,
      And, ere thy longing tires,
      Kindles His sudden fires.
Look, and let all thy soul be satisfied !

AFTER A RETREAT

WHAT hast thou learnt to-day?
    Hast thou sounded awful mysteries,
    Hast pierced the veilèd skies,
Climbed to the feet of God,
Trodden where saints have trod,
Fathomed the heights above?
        Nay,
This only have I learnt, that God is love.

What hast thou heard to-day?
Hast heard the Angel-trumpets cry,
And rippling harps reply;
Heard from the Throne of flame
Whence God incarnate came
Some thund'rous message roll?
        Nay,
This have I heard, His voice within my soul.

What hast thou felt to-day?
The pinions of the Angel-guide
That standeth at thy side

In rapturous ardours beat,
Glowing, from head to feet,
In ecstasy divine ?
    Nay,
This only have I felt, Christ's hand in mine.

IN THE MONTH OF MAY

"HAIL Mary!" Gabriel whispered, as
        he dropt—
      A shining herald of the Holy Three.
"Hail Mary!" and the dying world half-stopt
      His sick, sin-laden breath
      In nestling Nazareth;
And singing cherubim looked down to see.

"Hail Mary!" See, the trembling of the air;
   The Presence moves about her soft as fire;
For righteousness and peace have kissèd there.
      And suddenly the Shrine
      Is bright with light Divine,
The Hope of Israel and the world's Desire.

He whom we sought came suddenly, and found
   His Temple clean from every spot of sin;
And all the world seems consecrated ground;
      Her prayers, like incense, rise;
      And see, her very eyes
Shine like twin tapers as the Lord comes in.

Where the four mystic Eden-rivers rise
   The Angel-guard, that stands above the vale
And keeps the gate of sunlit Paradise,
      Let fall his sword of flame
      And cried upon thy name,
"Hail Mary!" and the garden answered "Hail!"

Shouted the sons of God; the morning stars
   Sang once again, as when the Lord began
To build the hills with battlements and bars.
      Ah, what a cry there fell!—
      "JESUS, EMMANUEL,"
The Lord of Angels and the Son of Man!

"Hail Mary!" For the world remembers yet
   The Maiden Mother and the Holy Son;
Remembers! How can any child forget
      The hope of heaven and thee—
      Such stainless purity—
Sin conquered, and the reign of peace begun?

Remembers! Yea, if I remember not
   The joys of Nazareth and Bethlehem,
Yet can thy dolours never be forgot:
      Thy thorn-crowned Son and thee
      Set high on Calvary,
The whole world mourns for—and remembers them.

" Hail Mary ! " When the ungenerous sons of men
   Grieve at thy glory, strip thee of thy praise,
The beasts and birds take up the song again
      With carol shrill and high
      Of Maying melody :
" Hail Mary, Mary Maiden, full of grace !"

O Mother, take this verse and pray for me,
   Now and at my last hour, lest that the cost
Of my redemption, and thy charity,
      Be wasted on thy Child,
      O Mary undefiled,—
Lest grace be vanquished and a sinner lost !

WEDDING HYMN

FATHER, within Thy House to-day
    We wait Thy kindly love to see ;
    Since thou hast said in truth that they
Who dwell in love are one with Thee,
Bless those who for Thy blessing wait,
Their love accept and consecrate.

Dear Lord of love, whose Heart of Fire,
    So full of pity for our sin,
Was once in that Divine Desire
    Broken, Thy Bride to woo and win :
Look down and bless them from above
And keep their hearts alight with love.

Blest Spirit, who with life and light
    Didst quicken chaos to Thy praise,
Whose energy, in sin's despite,
    Still lifts our nature up to grace ;
Bless those who here in troth consent.
Creator, crown Thy Sacrament.

55

Great One in Three, of Whom are named
    All families in earth and heaven,
Hear us, who have Thy promise claimed,
    And let a wealth of grace be given ;
Grant them in life and death to be
Each knit to each, and both to Thee.

SAVONAROLA MORITURUS

DEATH ! It is death, dear death, whom I
   sought so long
  On the rack, on the stairs, in the cell,
Death that I feared, half-feared, when my brain
  was strong,
   And my heart was well.
Now I am sickened of life, if life be this,
  Death comes as dear as a bride ;
Dying is rest from the flesh, and dying is bliss
   With Thee at my side.

" Faint heart, poor soul," do they say, " to recant
  at a pain,
  To repent at the turn of a screw ! "
Ah, I ask pardon of God again and again,
   And pardon from you !
Can the brain balance and weigh when the sinews
  are rent,
  Is there room but for agony there ?
What if the lips have lied, did the heart consent
   In that night of despair ?
Slow rocked the rafters above as I blinked in my
  pain

With the tears and the sweat in my eyes ;
Torn was my heart on the rack, and entangled my
brain ;
Is there cause for surprise ?

Visions ! what visions ? I know not, but leave
them to Him
Who allowed me to dream of a day
When a world that is weary with sorrow, whose
longings are dim
And dumb with delay,
Shall look to this city and cry for that secret of hers
That should shine in her eyes, on her lips.
Nay, but I dreamed of too much ! the wisest man
errs,
The surest foot slips.
Yet is it wonder I dreamed that the King of the sky
Should be King of the earth that He trod ?
Nay, He was King for a moment in Florence, and I
Gave glory to God.

Yea, is it wonder I dreamed that the Saviour could
save,
As I saw in the twilight below
God's light a-glimmer on faces in transept and nave ?
Who could know, who could know

Soon—ah so soon—that the glimmer would change
    to a glare
    And the stillness to noisy contempt—
Nave where they listened would yield to the
    bellowing square,
        And the dream that I dreamt
Fade in this bitter awakening ?   Bitter the ban
    Of the Church that I love.   Yet I cry
Mercy of God : for the mercies or curses of man
        Shall be nought by and by.
Naked I came from Him, naked return I again
    To my God through a fiery door ;
Back, earth to earth, go I through a portal of pain.
        Can friar do more ?

HERO WORSHIP

ALMOST a very god thou wert to me ;
  Haloed with brilliant virtues ; every grace
  Lived in thy look and shone about thy face :
I bowed beneath thee, loved, feared, worshipped
    thee.
Then in my folly and my jealousy
  I let my critic thoughts prevail apace,
  Which entered, swarming, tore thee from thy
    place,
And dashed thee down in wrath and enmity.

So some ungallant priest in other days
  Bade Cromwell's troopers to the House of God,
    And marked Our Lady totter from the height ;
And when the shame was finished, in amaze
  Looked piteously, and, kneeling where they trod,
    Fell all a-weeping at the sorry sight.

LAUDA SION SALVATOREM

LAUD, O Sion, thy Salvation,
    Laud in songs of exultation
        This thy Shepherd and thy King :
All thy might in triumph raising
Praise Him who surpasses praising,
    Far beyond thine honouring.

Be our theme of high thanksgiving
Living Bread and source of living
    Set to-day before us here :—
Broken at that Supper blessed,
As by every mouth confessed,
    For the brethren gathered there.

Laud be lifted, sweet and sounding,
Ringing from an heart abounding,
    Rising into jubilee !
Laud in duteous celebration
Of this Table's consecration
    For such high solemnity.

Lo, the King His Law revises ;
Newer truth from elder rises,
    Newer Law and Paschal rite.

Ancient truths their room surrender,
Glows the twilight into splendour,
    Darkness vanishes in light.

That He wrought at supper lying
In remembrance of His dying
    Christ hath bid His Church renew ;
We the ordinance obeying,
Earthly bread and wine displaying,
    Consecrate the Victim due.

Now the sacred truth receiving
We,—the Bread His Flesh believing
    And the Wine His Blood to be,
What tho' eye and mind be failing,
Nature's order countervailing—
    Grasp by faith the mystery.

Under diverse kinds concealed
While to sense yet unrevealed
    Lies a wonder all-divine.
Flesh and Blood hath each its token
Yet abides their Christ unbroken
    Hidden under either sign.

Perfect to the priest who breaks it,
Perfect in the hand that takes it,
    Christ is undivided there.

One or thousands may receive Him
Yet true hearts in truth believe Him
　　Unconsuměd everywhere.

Good and bad alike partaking
Each, by diverse lot, is making
　　One to woe and one to weal,
Each from each is set asunder :
Mark the word of grace and wonder—
　　One to hurt and one to heal.

Thus the Lord His Presence hiding
Dwells in many parts abiding,—
Every soul in Him confiding
　　Doubts not that the Whole is there.
He the One remaineth ever
Under every part : for never
Aught can Christ from Christ dissever,
　　Still abiding everywhere.

CHRISTIAN EVIDENCES

NOW God forbid that Faith be blind assent,
    Grasping what others know ; else Faith
      were nought
But learning, as of some far continent
      Which others sought,
And carried thence, better the tale to teach,
Pebbles and shells, poor fragments of the beach.

Now God forbid that Faith be built on dates,
    Cursive or uncial letters, scribe or gloss,
What one conjectures, proves, or demonstrates :
      This were the loss
Of all to which God bids that man aspire,
This were the death of life, quenching of fire.

Nay, but with Faith I see.   Not even Hope,
    Her glorious sister, stands so high as she.
For this but stands expectant on the slope
      That leads where He
Her source and consummation sets His seat,
Where Faith dwells always to caress His Feet.

Nay, but with Faith I saw my Lord and God
    Walk in the fragrant garden yesterday.

Ah! how the thrushes sang; and, where He trod
        Like spikenard lay
Jewels of dew, fresh-fallen from the sky,
While all the lawn rang round with melody.

Nay, but with Faith I marked my Saviour go,
  One August noonday, down the stifling street
That reeked with filth and man; marked from Him
    flow
        Radiance so sweet,
The man ceased cursing, laughter lit the child,
The woman hoped again, as Jesus smiled.

Nay, but with Faith I sought my Lord last night,
  And found Him shining where the lamp was dim;
The shadowy altar glimmered, height on height,
      A throne for Him:
Seen as through lattice work His gracious Face
Looked forth on me and filled the dark with grace.

Nay then, if proof and tortured argument
  Content thee—teach thee that the Lord is there,
Or risen again; I pray thee be content,
     But leave me here
With eye unsealed by any proof of thine,
With eye unsealed to know the Lord is mine.

E   65

Prove if thou wilt, my friend, that Paul is Paul
   And Peter Peter : talk till crack of doom ;
Marshal thy facts ; yes, yes, I know them all ;
         And, spite of gloom,
Of all the dust and science raised by thee,
I saw my Lord was there Who smiled on me.

Thou dost believe that, ah, so long ago
   He lived, wrought marvels, and was crucified,
Because that Holy Matthew tells thee so ?
         I, on my side,
Know Him as Love ; and Love could not pass by
And leave men sinning—therefore Love must die.

Thou dost believe, because He rose again,
   That Christ is very God ? Yet I believe
He rose because I see Him walk with men,
         Sinners receive,
Loose stammering tongues, open the blindest eyes.
And none but God doth so ; and God must rise.

"Nay, but I serve Him," is thy claim, "for yet
   The faith of some rests all on evidence.
Men will remember me, while they forget
         Thine eloquence,
And set it by for solid argument ;
Let me serve such, and I am well content."

66

Each to his own : yet surely I have read
   How of two sisters (each to Him was dear),
One listened but to what the Saviour said,—
         Thought to be near
The Lord Himself were best :—the other ran
Laid plates, clashed dishes, filled and set the can ;

And all to serve Him.   Yet the Lord preferred
   A quiet face, and that turned up to read
The reason of His silence or His word ;
         And said indeed
Somewhat, I fancy, of a better part
Near to His Feet, but nearer to His Heart.

Choose thou, then, Martha, if thou wilt ; perchance
   The joy of serving is enough for thee.
Let me choose Mary ; yea, love's arrogance
         Is all for me :
Nay, more than Mary—let me seek His side
And sit by Him in penitential pride.

THE PRIEST'S LAMENT

LORD, hast thou set me here
        Thy priest to be,
      The burden of Thy yoke to bear,
To feel thy cords about me set,
Wince at the lash, but never yet
        Thy Face to see?

Lord, see what wounds on me
        Thy burden makes!
Dost Thou despise my misery?
Ah, Master! wilt Thou let me strain,
And fall and rise and fall again,
        Till my heart breaks?

Lord, I am near to die,
        So steep the hill,
So slow the wheels, so feeble I,
The halting place so far above.
Art Thou indeed a God of Love,
        And tender still?

THE PRIEST'S LAMENT

" Son, turn a moment, see
Is that blood thine ?
Who is it shares thy yoke with thee,
Treads foot by foot with thee the road ?
Whose shoulder bears the heavier load,—
Is it not Mine ? "

IN THE GARDEN OF A RELIGIOUS HOUSE

SEE, how the sombre cassocks come and go,
  About the sunny garden, in and out !
  God reigns in highest heaven—while here
    below
      We grope and rout ;
And, like our foolish fathers down the ages,
Look for divinity in printed pages.

" Look at that priest, how slow he walks, how slow !
  You would not think he ran a race with Death ;
Why does he loiter here ?   Rise, rise and go,
      Draw swifter breath !
Go ! let your pulses leap with love and laughter ;
Live now ! and let God settle what comes after !

" Mark that man—how he moves with nervous
    speed ;
  His blood is beating hot in heart and brain ;
Ah, cast away that cold and cruel creed !
      Go back again
Tear off that black ; and leap and ride and run,
And live like Adam in the wind and sun !

70

" What, does God love to see his creatures pine,
   Crouching and cringing—weaklings half-afraid ?
God, who has made the oil, the wheat, the vine,
        Bright sun, cool shade,
God, who has fashioned youth, clean limbs, red
   blood.
What, said He not that all is very good ? "

So spoke the Devil in me, as I sat
   To watch the brethren passing to and fro.
So he had whispered, till I fancied that
        Myself said so :
That it was I that chafed and longed to flee
And taste, with God's consent, such liberty.

Then dropt a sudden sickness on my heart,
   That shook it, as an ague shakes a limb.
I marked a lean priest as he walked apart,
        And feared for him :
So once men trembled when they saw on high
Hung on a Cross a God in agony.

Ah ! not with wealth and wine and gaiety
   Did God bring back His wayward human race.
There was no beauty there for us to see
        In that marred Face,
When God Incarnate passed from Pilate's hall,
Bearing the heavy Cross to save us all.

71

No gracious woman leaned and laughed ; no child
   Clapped gladsome hands to speed Him to that
     Hill ;
Only the piteous Mother undefiled
       Stared white and still
On Him Who knew her pains and pitied them,
With all the daughters of Jerusalem.

Thus Adam's sin, that ruined Adam's seed,
   And shut the gate that leads to Paradise,
Was ransomed by that bitter price decreed—
      Christ's Sacrifice—
When Satan sickened, and the old world died
Beneath the sad eyes of the Crucified.

The Crucified !   And thus His servant spoke :
  "Whereby the world is crucified to me,
And I unto the world."   The darkness broke,
      And, fair to see,
The garden shone—the priests went to and fro.
God has gone up, but left His Cross below.

A CHRISTMAS CAROL

THERE went a merry company
    On the road to Bethlehem,
    Going all to taxèd be
By the governour's decree
    On the road to Bethlehem—
Would I had been there to see.
Would I had been there to see
    On the road to Bethlehem ;
Mary, Joseph, pray for me !

Coldly blew the wind and snow
    On the road to Bethlehem.
Two there were that walkèd slow,
All that day so long ago,
    On the road to Bethlehem ;
Would I had been there also.
Would I had been there to see
    On the road to Bethlehem ;
Mary, Joseph, pray for me !

One, a maid of high degree,
    On the road to Bethlehem,
Walking, walking wearily ;—

" Joseph—Joseph, wait for me
    On the road to Bethlehem ! "
Would I had been there to see.
Would I had been there to see
    On the road to Bethlehem ;
Mary, Joseph, pray for me !

Thus they came the town within,
    To the town of Bethlehem ;
Sought they straight the public inn,
So they might a shelter win
    In the town of Bethlehem ;
See them tirling at the pin.
Would I had been there to see
    On the road to Bethlehem ;
Mary, Joseph, pray for me !

"Get you gone—the night is late
    In the town of Bethlehem."
Hear them chapping at the gate,
Richer folk both small and great,
    In the town of Bethlehem—
When *they* knock the poor must wait.
Would I had been there to see
    On the road to Bethlehem ;
Mary, Joseph, pray for me !

Sought they straight the stable door
    In the town of Bethlehem.
Mary dropped upon the floor ;
Wearied was she—wearied sore
    In the town of Bethlehem.
" Joseph dear—I can no more."
Would I had been there to see
    On the road to Bethlehem ;
Mary, Joseph, pray for me !

" Cheer thee, cheer thee, Mary Maid,
    In the town of Bethlehem—
See the straw is smoothly laid."
Poor folks' wages, poorly paid,
    In the town of Bethlehem !
Would I had been there to aid.
Would I had been there to see
    On the road to Bethlehem ;
Mary, Joseph, pray for me !

What a lodging, cold and bare,
    In the town of Bethlehem.
Bring me wrappings fine and fair,
Silk and satin rich and rare,
    In the town of Bethlehem—
Lay our Lady softly there !

Would I had been there to see
    On the road to Bethlehem ;
Mary, Joseph, pray for me !

Nay, no silk or satin bright
    In the town of Bethlehem !
Think ye on this wondrous sight
Soon to see : The Lord of Light
    In the town of Bethlehem
Comes in lowliness to-night.
Would I had been there to see
    On the road to Bethlehem ;
Mary, Joseph, pray for me !

Ox and ass with patient pace,
    In the town of Bethlehem,
Mark the Maiden full of grace
Lying by the manger-place
    In the town of Bethlehem—
Lying in such sorry case.
Would I had been there to see
    On the road to Bethlehem ;
Mary, Joseph, pray for me !

Ere the night had passed to morn,
    In the town of Bethlehem,
Rose the Sun on us forlorn ;

In the manger old and worn,
    In the town of Bethlehem,
Jesus Christ our Lord was born.
Would I had been there to see
    On the road to Bethlehem ;
Mary, Joseph, pray for me !

Eastern Kings are on their way
    To the town of Bethlehem ;
Shepherds run ere break of day
At His Feet their vows to pay
    In the town of Bethlehem,
Where a God Incarnate lay.
Would I had been there to see
    On the road to Bethlehem ;
Mary, Joseph, pray for me !

Christian souls, with one accord
    Come to Holy Bethlehem ;
Meet Him at His Holy Board ;
Praise the Saviour, praise the Lord,—
    In the town of Bethlehem
Who on us His glory poured !
Would I had been there to see
    In the town of Bethlehem ;
Mary, Joseph, pray for me !

AVE VERUM CORPUS NATUM

HAIL, true Body born of Mary,
    Which for man was crucified;
    Lo, the mingled blood and water,
Flowing from the piercèd Side!

Lord of Life Who once did'st suffer,
    When we draw our latest breath,
Be to us our Food and succour
    In the awful hour of death!

APPENDIX

APPENDIX

LAST DAYS

Canon Sharrock, *of Salford Cathedral, supplies the following account of Mgr. Benson's last days and death:*

MONSIGNOR BENSON wrote on September 22 (1914) that he was unwell and, in view of the fact that he had promised to preach a course of sermons in Salford Cathedral during the month of October, bade me to be prepared for a telegram in case his medical adviser declared his condition serious. "I write this," he said, "in case you receive a sudden telegram, and I trust you will not imagine me either dilatory or perverse." He wrote a second letter, saying he had seen his doctor, who declared that the pains were symptoms of "false angina," and, whilst painful, were not of a serious character. He was permitted to continue his work.

I did not see him on October 4, the first Sunday of October, when he preached, as I was away from home; but I was informed that he appeared somewhat unwell. He proceeded on Monday, October 5, to Ulverston, and gave a week's mission there. On

F

the Saturday evening of October 10 I met him at Victoria Station, Manchester, and was struck at once by his changed condition. He appeared incapable of moving with his usual briskness, and stopped every few steps to inhale deep breaths to alleviate the sudden pain. He was quite confident that the distress was only of a temporary character, as his heart had been pronounced quite sound. He found the ascent of stairs very trying, and mounted with great slowness. Every expression of anxiety on my part was met with great confidence that the pain, though severe, was of no consequence. In spite of all remonstrances and entreaties, he resolutely declined my request that he should rest and give up his work at the Cathedral and elsewhere for the month of October. With that politeness ever his wont he thrust my objections aside. He preached on the Sunday evening of October 11. His sermon was a little longer than usual, though I observed the absence of his usual animation. On his return to the sacristy, he was obliged to rest for a considerable time in a chair. He soon recovered, however, and retired to rest somewhat earlier than usual, wishful to make up for the great loss of sleep he had experienced during the week owing to the pain.

After an awful night of pain and great restlessness, he decided to leave for London on Monday,

October 12, by the early morning train. We had not gone many yards towards the station when he bade me stop the taxi, and drive to the nearest doctor, as he could bear the pain no longer. With great difficulty I got him back to the house, and sent for the nearest doctor, who came immediately. Examination resulted in the previous verdict being endorsed, and remedies were presented. It was deemed advisable to cancel all engagements for the present, though the Monsignor suspended his judgement in the matter. The pain yielded to treatment and a quiet day was passed. After two hours' sleep that night, the excruciating pain returned with greater violence and continued all Tuesday without cessation. Tuesday night and Wednesday morning saw no relief, and a specialist was invited to share the responsibility of the medical attendant. A long examination resulted in the endorsement of the previous decision, but the pain still continued for some time, and yielded to treatment about Wednesday noon. He then took to bed, and presumably was on his way to the recovery of sleep. He obtained broken sleep through Wednesday night. Congestion of the right lung began to show itself on Thursday, and in spite of the continued attendance of the specialist and doctor, by Thursday night was highly developed. Still no danger was anticipated, and his splendid vitality was deemed sufficient to throw off the indisposition.

Real danger became manifest on Friday, and Saturday saw little change. It was deemed advisable to prepare him for the worst eventuality, but he himself had full confidence in his strength of recuperation. He received the Last Rites with great devotion and all unbidden made his Profession of Faith with marked strength and vivacity. Sunday morning saw a change after a restless night which had tried the endurance of both doctor and nurse. He was never delirious, but his restlessness was acute. On Sunday morning I gave him Holy Viaticum. His piety and devotion were most touching. He made all the responses, even correcting me when my emotion caused me to stumble at the " Misereatur."

On Sunday morning he received a visit from his brother (Mr. Arthur C. Benson), which gave him great pleasure. He even then informed me that he would be quite well by Tuesday, "though," he added, "this hard breathing is a terrible bore." His mental faculties were as keenly active as ever, and no tendency to mental exhaustion was observable. His strength appeared good, but it was only too evident that the terrible strain on the heart from the pneumonia was beginning to tell. Later on, in the evening, for the first time, I abandoned hope. He spoke continually to me of his friends, and gave me his many messages.

At one o'clock on Monday morning, having left him for a short time, I was hastily summoned by the nurse, at his request. Entering the sick room, I saw that the last call had come. He told me so himself, with the words, "God's will be done." He bade me summon his brother, who was in the adjoining apartment. The prayers for the dying were recited, and again he joined in the responses, clearly and distinctly. Once when I paused he bade me in God's name to go on. He stopped the prayers twice or thrice to give some instructions to his brother. He asked once for guidance as to the right attitude towards death. Once, as I paused, he uttered the prayer, "Jesus, Mary and Joseph, I give you my heart and my soul," and joined with us in its completion. Conscious almost to the last moment, seemingly without pain, he breathed forth his soul without struggle at 1.30 A.M. on Monday morning. With his eyes fixed on the priest he died; it was just as if he had gone to sleep.

The Publishers are indebted to the Editor of THE TABLET *for leave to reproduce this communication and portions of the Prefatory Note from his columns.*

Sept 26. 1914

My dear Norman,

I do indeed wish every success
to the appeal that M. René
Bazin is making for your boys.
I am delighted to think that I
have known your work significantly
in the years in which we were
both Protestants, & continuously
ever since: & have known, even
in detail, what a splendid work it is.
I am certain that it has only to be

made known to a few more
charitable people, to be set
for ever beyond the reach of
anxiety.

Yours ever affectionately

Robert Hugh Benson

FACSIMILE OF ROBERT HUGH BENSON'S WRITING
A letter written a few days before his death to
Mr. Norman Potter

PRINTED AT
THE BALLANTYNE PRESS
LONDON & EDINBURGH